Pun Times

OFFSHOOT

A pun-tastic activity book

First edition 2018
Offshoot Books
An imprint of Kalabindu Enterprises Pvt. Ltd

GF–18, Virat Bhavan
Commercial Complex, Mukherjee Nagar
Delhi 110009
Phone: +91-11-47038000 / Fax: +91-11-47038099
Website: www.offshootbooks.com

Dear Reader,

Thank you for buying this book. We hope you enjoy every page of the book—and while you do that, please ensure that no one uses or transmits any part of this publication, in any form or by any means, without our prior written permission. You wouldn't want to offend the no-offence brand.

In case we haven't mentioned it before, we truly think that you are our favorite reader. Thanks for being a part of the Offshoot universe.

Have fun!

Love,
Team Offshoot

ISBN: 978-93-86362-49-0
Printed in India
Picture credits: www.shutterstock.com

Many a time, people will tell you,
Puns are tearable, but that's not true!
They whale pursuade you to think so too,
If you disagree, they will pun-ish you!

Famous people have shunned puns,
Said that they are no fun.
But the Bard swore by them,
Used them for satire and even for mayhem.

We can assure you that they have a higher porpoise,
For humor, they are a great choice.
Don't believe what we say?
This book will change your mind, have a good day!

LET THE PUN BEGIN

Think you are clever?

Use the clues to form words, without a single error.

No

Hint: They can see through you.

Plum

Hint: They go deep to fix the problem.

Law

Hint: They look down on people.

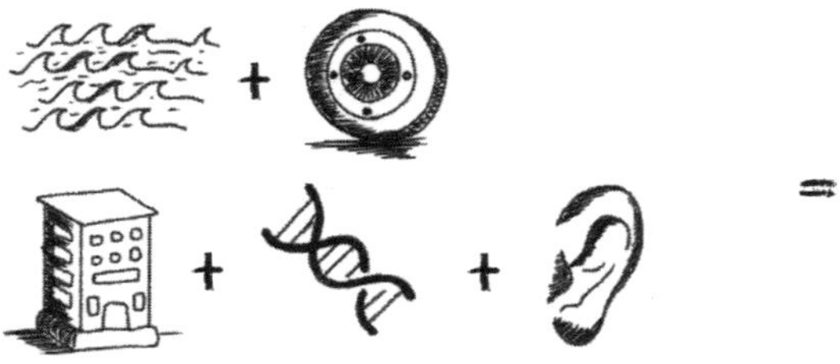

Inn

Hint: They only believe in concrete evidence.

Hint: They know more about you than you do.

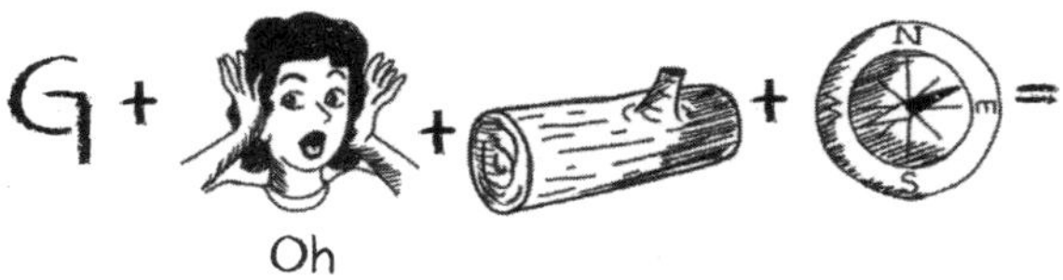

Hint: They can rock the world.

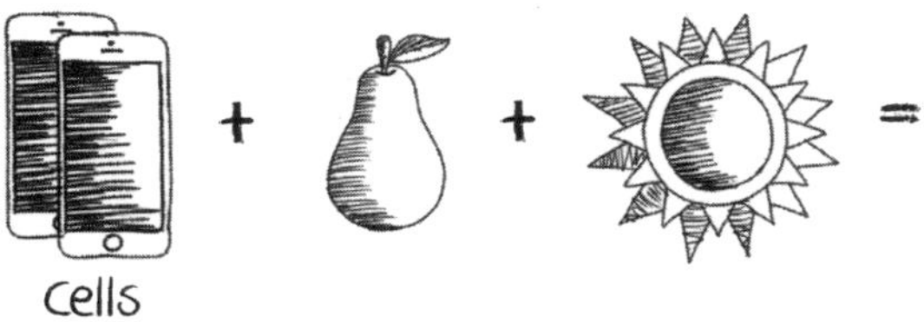

Hint: They understand one's needs very well.

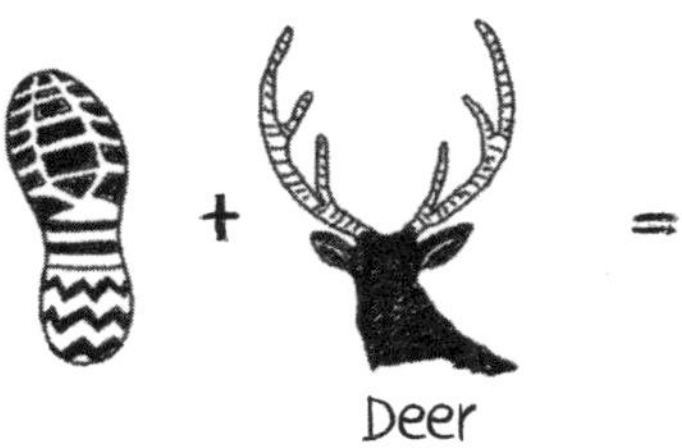

Hint: The duty-full citizens of a country.

What did the frog work as at the hotel?

A bellhop!

The puzzle is simple, don't break your bones. Fill in the blanks, then solve the crossword with homophones.

Across

2. I am not always _____, but I am never wrong.
3. Are we _____ yet?
4. _____ me out!
7. Oh! You're dead _____!

Down

1. _____ one do you prefer?
2. Fire in the _____.
5. My dog _____ my homework!
6. _____ in the headlights.

Turn around for a break

Egg, jam, toast and butter form the
breakfast club,
one of each is hiding below, spot and
circle the grub!

So many puns, now do something fun.

A smile brightens up your face,
board the molar express, and
trace a-maize!

And the fun continues...

The beginning, middle and end have puns, guesstimate the words and have some fun!

1. __ PUN
2. PUN__ __H
3. E__ PUN__E
4. C__ __ PUNC__I__N
5. __C__ PUNC__U__E
6. PUN__T__ __T__ __N
7. C__B__RPUN__
8. PUN__T__ __L

Hints

1. Woven
2. Penalize
3. Remove
4. Reluctance
5. Chinese treatment for ailments
6. Marks used in writing
7. Programmer
8. On time

You have a list of chores to crack,
Put them all under a-tack!

What does a thesaurus have for breakfast?

A synonym roll.

Start it with positivi-tea 

or expresso the way you want 

The signages below use clever puns, can you guess them for everyone?

We will heel you,
We will save your sole,
We will even dye for you!

____

Hint: They repair what is beneath you.

Hint: The room delivers good news.

Push. Push. Push.

____

We would be delighted if you send in your payment on time. However, if you don't, you will be de-lighted.

____

Hint: Their knowledge may shock you.

Don't stand there and be hungry; come on in and get fed up.

____

Hint: The place waits for orders.

If you don't see what you're looking for, you've come to the right place.

____

Hint: He helps you see everything.

The best way to get back on your feet—miss a car payment.

____

Hint: They get things moving.

Is the journey a very long one?
Find all the words related to pun!

P	W	L	W	Q	B	P	X	A	P	A	M
T	G	I	O	A	M	U	U	B	X	D	J
R	E	P	T	I	N	N	U	E	N	D	O
R	Y	G	P	T	P	B	E	N	G	W	K
Q	E	D	P	P	I	P	P	D	T	I	E
Q	U	I	B	B	L	E	P	L	P	T	B
U	W	E	R	T	Y	U	I	P	P	T	C
I	S	D	F	D	H	G	B	S	B	I	F
P	X	C	B	S	N	D	N	N	M	C	D
T	O	M	F	O	O	L	E	R	Y	I	A
P	A	A	L	P	A	F	A	M	D	S	P
W	I	S	E	C	R	A	C	K	P	M	B

Find these words

PUN, INNUENDO, JOKE, QUIBBLE, QUIP,
WITTICISM, WISECRACK, TOMFOOLERY

Turn around for a break

When a pun just isn't fun...

When 'dead' lines haunt you day and night, take a break and play this right!

Instructions

1. The game can be played by two or more people.
2. The players can join 2 adjacent dots using horizontal or vertical lines.
3. The player who completes the fourth side of a 1×1 box, can color it and take another turn.
4. The player with maximum number of boxes wins the game.

The dead lines chase you during the daytime too, meet them head-on before they say 'Boo'!

Do this activity for fun.

Reading books can be a shellfish activity.
Cut out the bookmark to tag the page,
and carry on with friends or family.

JUST

BELIEVE

IN

YOUR

SHELF!

OFFSHOOT

You are booked for most part of the week,
name some of your favorite titles,
the ones you often seek.

Informal language is called slang,
Look at the illustrations to get the hang.

1. Hint: To make a mistake, or mess up.

____

2. Hint: A lazy person who spends the bulk of his time lazing on a couch.

____

3.

Hint: To casually gather together or spend time with someone in a social manner.

4.

Hint: A metaphor for binge eating.

5.

Hint: An adjective for practicality and lack of pretence.

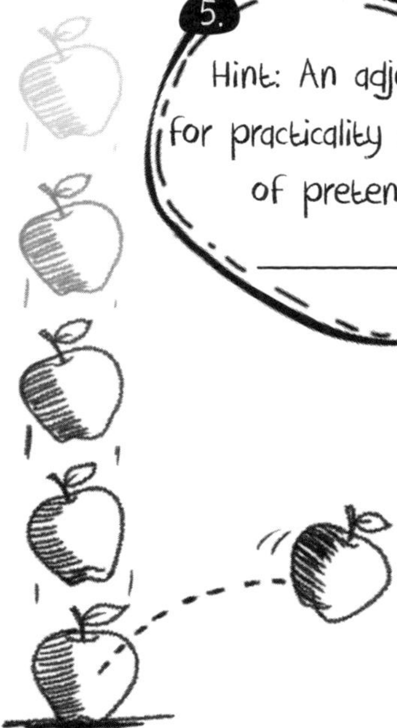

1 What do you call twin brothers?

____

Hint: Dusk

2 What did the buffalo say to his son when he left for college?

____

Hint: Farewell

3 What does a clock do when it's hungry?

____

Hint: It's a matter of few moments.

Tap your head and tickle your bones, read the question and guess the homophones!

4 What did the baby corn ask mama corn?

____

Hint: It's golden and buttery.

5 What is the golf club's favorite kind of music?

____

Hint: It's groovy!

6 Why are movie stars so cool?

____

Hint: They are crazy about them.

Turn around for a break

Time for a punny 'brake'.

If you're fed up with too many puns,
brake for a break,
play tic-tac-toe with anyone!

Pluggy's current behavior was appalling, to conduct well, help him find his true calling.

And so it continues.

The conversation of two book lovers is not so funny. They discussed a book, now make it punny!

A: I am reading a book on anti-gravity. It's difficult to put ________.

B: Is the theme of the book ________?

A: It's great! The message is actually ________ on me.

B: How is the narrative? Is it gripping or does it ________ away?

A. That's the brilliant part. You never know when it ________ in completely.

B: So, it is marketed towards more substantial ________.

A: Yes, it's commercial. But there is ________ for introspection and imagination.

B: As long as it does not ______________ of story-writing.

Grammar Nazis, please assemble!
Guess the answer and make 'em tremble.

1. What happened when the Past, Present and Future walked into the bar?

   It was ____________.

2. Why are apostrophes terrible to date?

   Because they are too ____________.

3. Which dinosaur knows a lot of synonyms?

   It is called a ____________.

4. Why do words, phrases and punctuations keep ending up in court?

   To be ____________.

5. What's the best way to get an English major in the mood?

________ - play

6. What's the difference between a cat and a comma?

One has ________ at the end of its paws and the other has a ________ at the end of a clause.

7. What is the meaning of this?

It's a ________.

Decipher the grid and complete the words, to solve the famous puns written by the Bard!

What do you call an alligator in a vest?

An Investigator.

Key

A		N	13
B		O	
C		P	
D	23	Q	10
E		R	
F		S	
G		T	
H		U	
I	18	V	
J		W	
K		X	3
L		Y	
M		Z	

7	12

25	22

12	9

13	12	7

7	12

25	22

7	19	26	7

18	8

7	19	22

10	6	22	8	7	18	12	13

Hint: Hamlet

2	12	6

19	26	5	22

23	26	13	24	18	13	20

8	19	12	22	8

4	18	7	19

13	18	14	25	15	22

8	12	15	22	8

18

19	26	5	22

26

8	12	6	15

12	21

15	22	26	23

Hint: Romeo and Juliet

Puns are great to test your friendship, complete the message chain below, use your pun-man-ship!

Turn around for a break

If you're bored of all the puns...

Circles are hot because they are 360 degrees, color the mandala to make it cool, please!

You have no Monet? Nowhere to Gogh?
Doodle on the van and lessen your woe!

Many words related to puns are in the cloud, find that one word which is the odd one out.

Take these puns very Literary,
Match the titles with their authors, hurry!

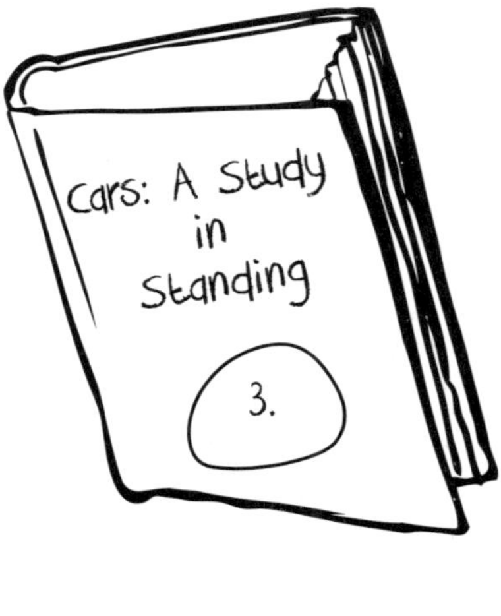

a. Hayley Tozies
b. Flour Parr
c. C. Quinn Ed.
d. Kole Meenor
e. D. Garrad Nerr
f. Parker D. Curr
g. Cramer Bruli
h. Burt Dender

Words with different meanings that sound similar, these are clues to make your task simpler.

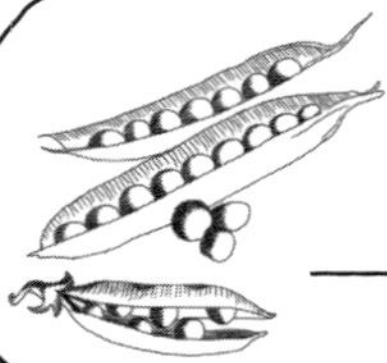

_____________ of mind.

_____________ do it.

____

to me,

this is right.

I _____________ you.

____

is precious.

_____________ of

approval.

Everything

____

be alright.

Let's _______________

about it.

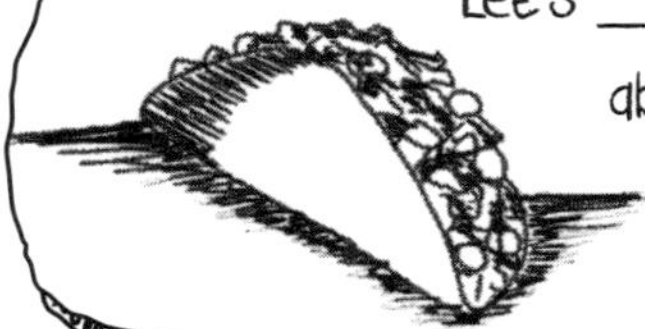

I did it on

_______________.

I am so

_______________.

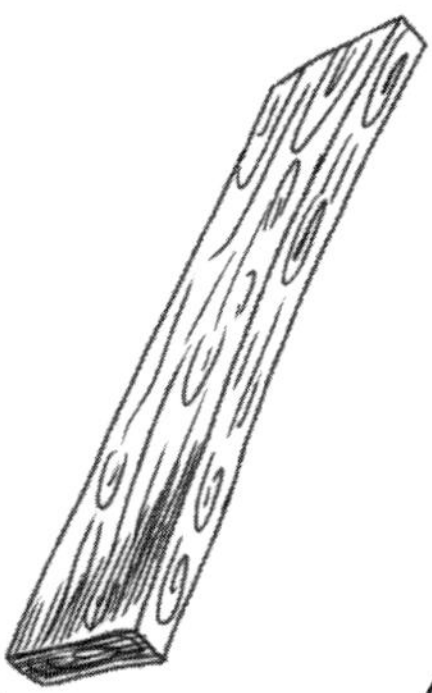

I love you

like no _______________.

You make my heart

_______________.

Homophones attack again!
Solve it quickly, it'll be your gain.

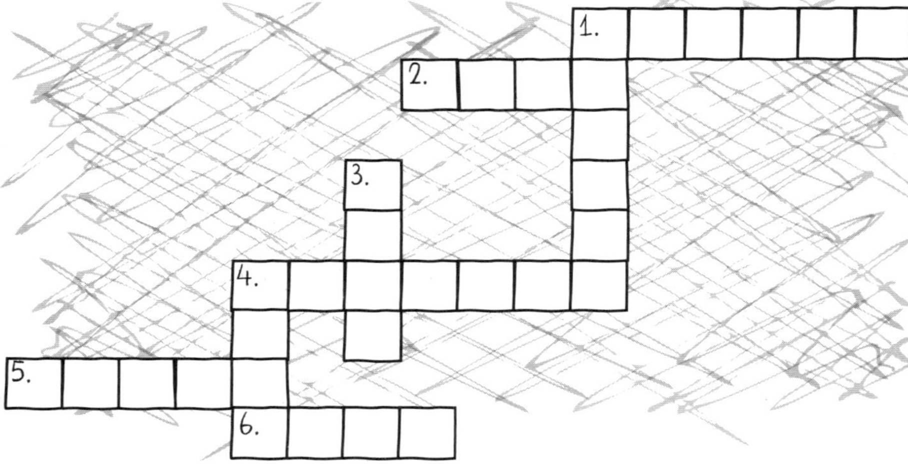

Across

1. I don't use the elevator, I always take the ______.
2. That's how I ______.
4. It's lovely ______.
5. Hippies rallied for world ______.
6. Do ______ enter.

Down

1. The ______ has a good collection of wine.
3. You can find anything at the ______ market.
4. I am unwell, and feeling ______.

Turn around for a break

Stop, pause and do this activity.

Spot the pi (π) before you have to eat
humble pie,
put them all in a circle,
make sure they catch your eye.

Note-books are musical as they have all the right notes.

Make a playlist of songs you love the most.

Time to stop!

Angry with someone or just want to mess around?
Cut out these pun-filled insults and act like a clown.

You get ten times more girls than me?
Ten times zero is zero...

There is no vaccine against stupidity.

You're the reason the gene pool needs a lifeguard.

Your argument is well-rounded,
which is why it's pointless.

You're hotter than me, because I am cooler than you.

God does make mistakes time and again.
Don't believe me? Look in the mirror for proof.

Your discussion about right and left was right.
Which is why I left.

If I were to climb on your ego and jump to your IQ,
I would die.

Of course I talk like an idiot, how else would you
understand me?

If you really spoke your mind, you'd be speechless.

Stupidity is not a crime so you are free to go.

OFFSHOOT

OFFSHOOT

OFFSHOOT

OFFSHOOT

OFFSHOOT

OFFSHOOT

OFFSHOOT

OFFSHOOT

OFFSHOOT

OFFSHOOT

OFFSHOOT

The pun candies are sweet to taste,
can you find the 'pon' one in haste?

Colorful answers will make your day,
using them, color the balloons and color away.

_______ you guys glad to see the land from this vantage point?

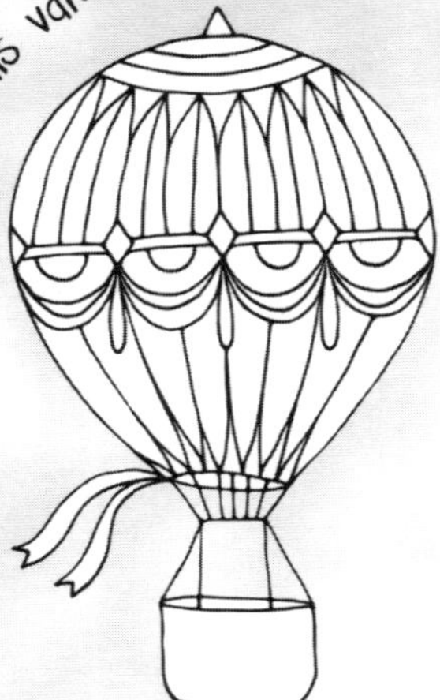

Oh! you _______ my mind.

The view just _______ my mind!

I am so happy that I am _______-ing like a fool.

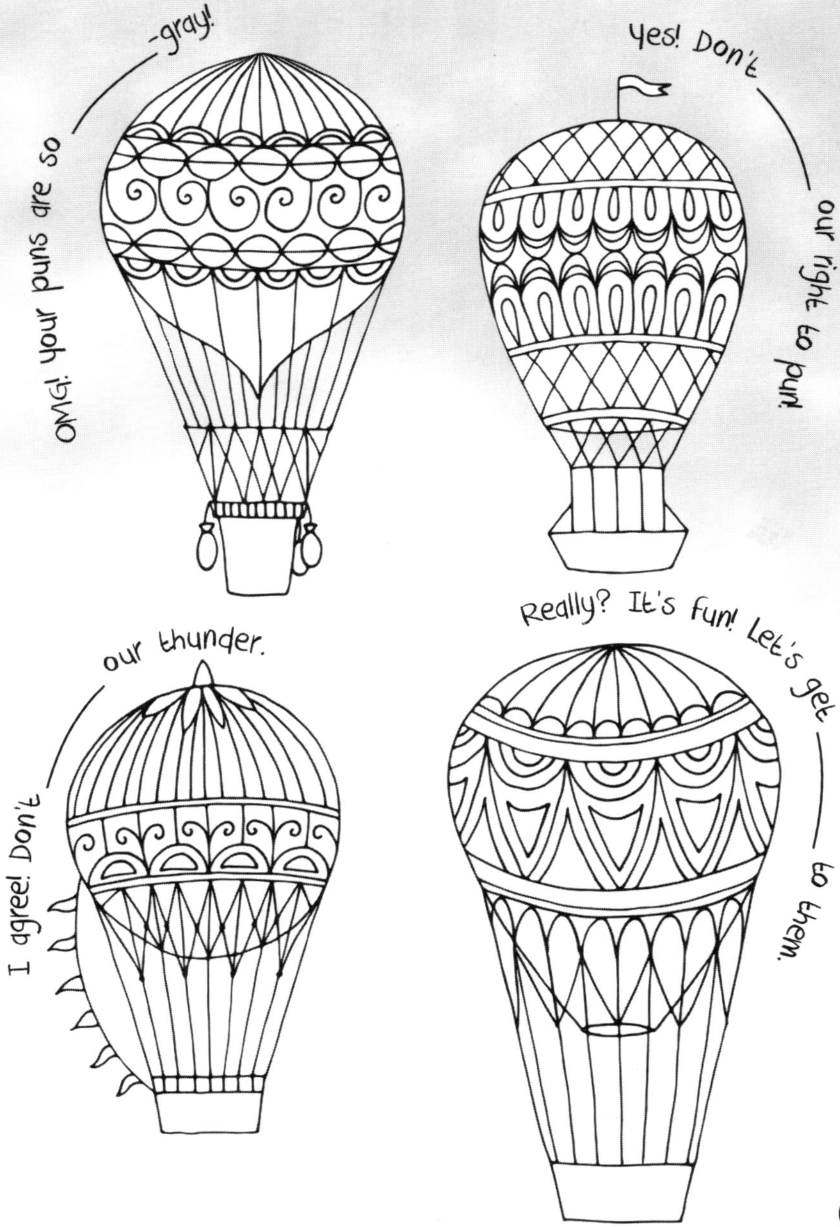

OMG! Your puns are so -gray!
Yes! Don't our right to pun!
I agree! Don't our thunder.
Really? It's fun! Let's get to them.

The flip-side of happiness can be sadness,
find the synonym of 'pun',
give in to the madness.

Turn around for a break

Stop and do this activity.

The mummy can't find its phone,
because it's all tied up.
Find it in the hieroglyphs, put its
world the right side up.

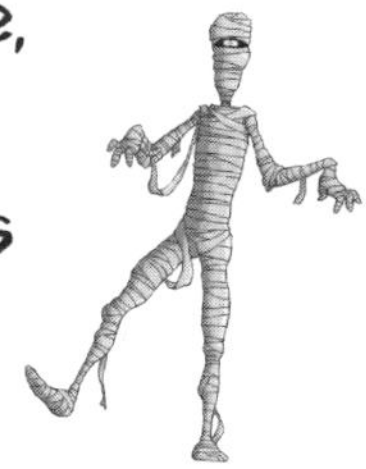

Feeling gray like the candies in the jar?
Find the one which is darker and bizarre!

Wordplay is what a pun is all about,
break the phrase below and cull more out.

P U N I N T E N D E D

Grammar puns attack again, See the clues and complete the chain!

1. Why are writers always cold? Because they're always surrounded by ________.

2. What did the period say to the sentence? We better ________ now!

3. Why is a book's plot so important? It ________ character.

4. Why did the book get thinner? It had its ___________ removed.

5. Hyperbole is without a doubt the ______________________ thing in the universe.

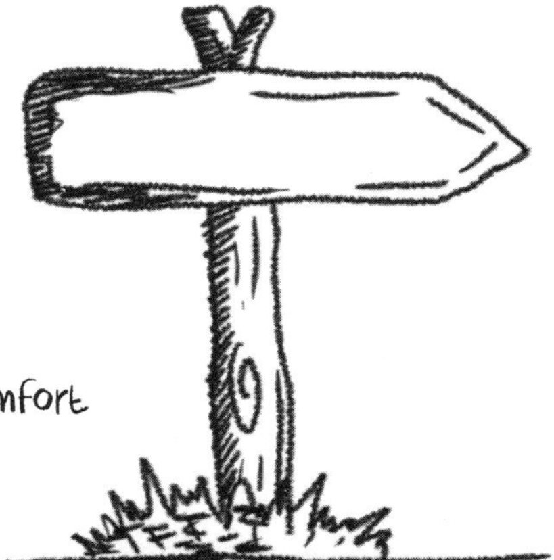

6. What do you say to comfort an English major? Their, they're, ___________.

Intention and message do not match,
spot the incorrect homophone in the batch!

1. WE SERVE PLANE AND CHEESE BURGERS HERE!

2. EXECUTIVE BORED ROOM

3. VIOLATORS SHALL BE FIND

4. THERE BACK

5. YOUR INVITED FOR THE SPECIAL EVENT

____

____

6. WE BYE USED CARS

____

____

7. PRIVATE PARKING. OTHER CARS WILL BE TOAD AWAY

____

____

____

8. MINED THE STEP

____

____

9. DO YOU NEED A BRAKE?

____

____

The two chemists have a hilarious reaction to lab gossip.

Formulate your answers well, it's an awesome topic.

Bro, Oxygen went for a date with Potassium, and it was ________.

Really? I was under the impression that Oxygen was dating Magnesium. ________!

No bro, I mean Oxygen did want to go out with Nitrogen, but Nitrogen was like ________

Oh damn! Oxygen wanted to go out with Sodium, but Sodium also said ________.

I hope when Oxygen goes out with Potassium again, it goes ________.

I do feel bad for Oxygen, when Oxygen was dumped by Hydrogen.

Yes, people shamed Oxygen by calling it a ________.

If it does not work out with Potassium, Oxygen should try to go out with Helium. It's ________

Turn around for a break

Don't tell a funny joke to the eggs,
they may crack up.
Color the eggs and their flowery backup.

Why not stop and color this?

Hop up, hop down, hop low, hop high,
help the bunny find the eggs before they dye.

And this one too.

Take a break and think about it, is this punny book enhancing your wit?

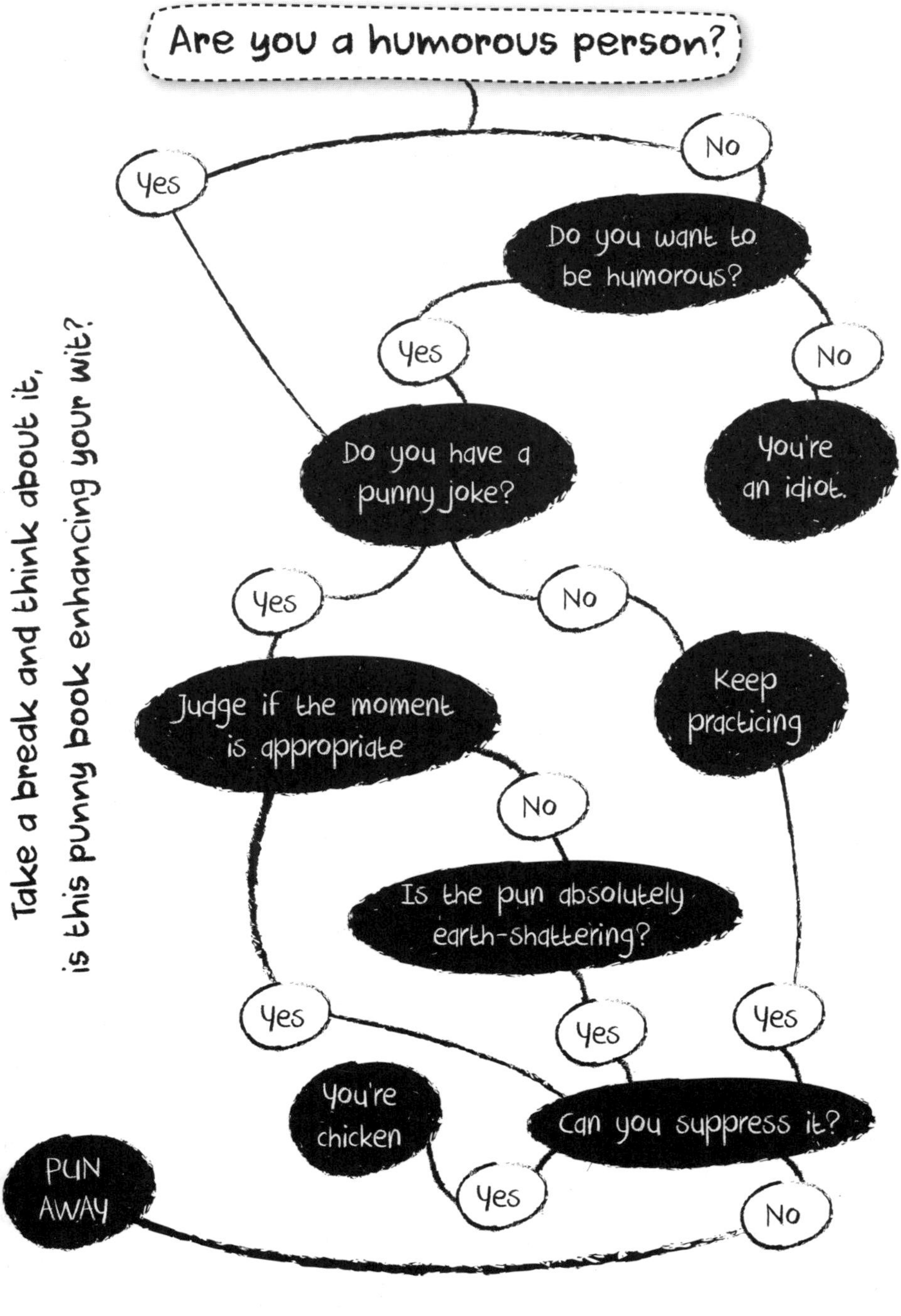

Want to touch a new note with your punning talent? Till you attempt these musical puns, you haven't.

What did the thief steal from the musical instrument store?

It was a ____________.

What did the turkey use to play his drums and win the competition?

His ____________.

What makes the pirates really good singers?

They manage to hit the high ____________!

What kind of music are bubbles and balloons scared of?

______ music.

Why was the singer locked out of his own house?

Because he struggled to find the right ______.

If a musician has a lot of problems, what will he be called?

A ______ man.

What happens when a pod of musical whales gather at a place?

______

Two people are having a hilarious conversation, fill in the blanks, and guess the names of the nations.

I am so ________,
I'm ________ die!

Hint: Capitals are Budapest; Accra

Ooh! I'll ________ it.

Hint: Helsinki's people

________ I'll do that!

Hint: Capital is Oslo

________ trust me?
________ my words, I will not fall sick.

Hint: Capitals are Nairobi; Copenhagen

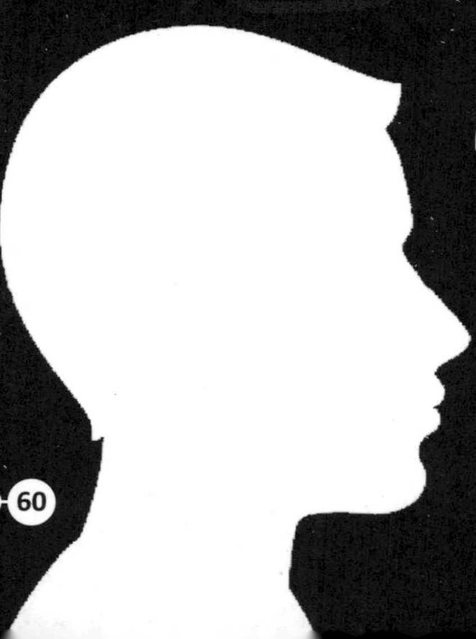

________ the refrigerator, there's some ________ there.

Hint: Capitals are Prague; Ankara

Cool! But don't ________ through it, otherwise you'll fall sick.

Hint: The place where Moscow is

I don't ________.

Hint: Capital is Sucre

Don't ________ to me later. ________ out of reasons to convince you.

Hint: Capitals are Madrid; Tehran

Think you know all the synonyms of pun? Search the words listed below one by one.

A	H	I	E	W	Z	N	E	V	A	B	S	W
P	M	D	S	Q	E	F	C	A	M	D	P	O
M	H	E	H	V	D	R	N	Q	B	W	E	M
B	O	O	T	G	E	R	P	H	I	V	E	B
E	P	P	M	A	U	O	Q	B	G	I	C	I
Z	H	H	G	O	P	R	U	N	U	P	H	N
Y	C	O	V	W	N	H	V	U	O	E	E	A
Z	Q	N	Y	W	L	Y	O	J	U	G	R	T
I	O	E	M	C	A	V	M	R	S	Y	R	I
M	E	T	O	N	Y	M	N	S	I	N	O	O
B	A	N	T	E	R	B	W	E	S	C	R	N

Find these words

IDEOPHONE, METAPHORIC, SPEECH ERROR, BANTER, HOMONYMS, AMBIGUOUS, WOMBINATION, METONYM

Turn around for a break

True mathematicians don't share numbers easily, but you can go through the puzzle breezily!

		3			6			
1		2	5				3	
	4		7		2	5		6
	5	1		2	7		8	
	9		8				4	7
				4		1		
2		7	9					
	8				5			9
	3		4			6		1

Pun is good till it lasts—after a while, the head blasts.

Math is the only subject that counts.
How many pencils are here, do recount!

Do this activity too.

The world of puns is an ocean of inspiration,
complete these gems and hang them at your workstation.

__________ the day.

Make __________.

Don't get __________ down.

Don't give into __________ pressure.

Don't be __________.

Be __________ sometimes.

Be __________ of yourself.

__________ the beauty of life.

OFFSHOOT

Complete the puns and fill in the blanks, change a letter in the answer to move up the ranks.

Chefs specializing in Chinese cuisine come from all woks of ___________.

She kept the wine glass on the top shelf in an attempt to ___________ her spirits.

After a night out, drinking wine with his mate, the pirate captain had a port ___________.

The investment banker had to resign, as he ___________ interest.

Ins-pun-rational quotes are fun and uplifting,
pen your own to keep the wok cooking and tossing.

Life's going nowhere.
Life's now-here.

No need to fill blanks or boxes for some time, simply recognize and circle the puns this time.

1. She had a photographic memory, but never developed it.

2. I was struggling to figure out how lightning works and then it struck me.

3. I really wanted a camouflage shirt, but I couldn't find one.

4. I've been to the dentist many times, so I know the drill.

5. How do construction workers party? They raise the roof.

6. A boiled egg every morning is hard to beat.

Turn around for a break

Are your puns scaring the people around you?

Write down your favorite horror flicks, name a few.

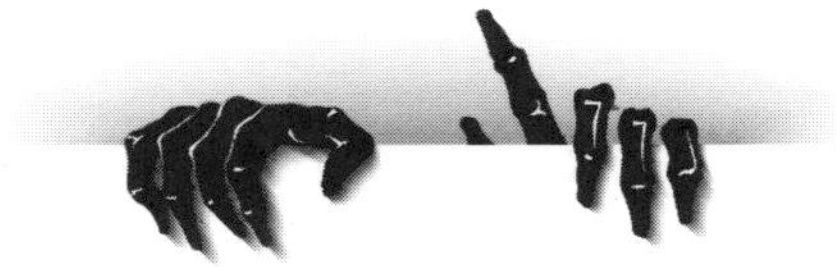

Just chill and do this for a thrill.

Color this too!

Solve this ladder here,
it is simple, have no fear.

The valet wanted to resign from his job, because he had no lot in __________.

I don't __________ stairs as they sometimes bring me down.

A cyclist rides his __________ in the morning and the evening, as he is a huge fan of recycling.

The yeast he could do to __________ a cake was to rise to the occasion.

Cows and bulls provide the raw material for various items of food.
Fill in the blanks with puns and improve your mooo-d!

Q. What do you call a cow with no legs?

A. ______________

Hint- It's minced meat.

Q. What do cows do for entertainment?

A. They go to ____________

Hint-It can be 3D or IMAX.

Q. What sort of band does a cow listen to?

A. ____________ Blues

Hint- It can go up or down.

Q. What is a sleeping bull called?

A. A ____________

Hint- Beware of him!!!

Q. Why can't cows keep a secret?

A. Because it will just go in one ear and out the

_____________.

Hint- You can really milk it.

Q. What do you call a cow that has just given birth?

A. _____________

Hint- The coffee
without caffeine.

Q. What's a bull's favorite kind of pasta?

A. _____________

Hint- It's meaty and tangy.

Q. What advice did the cow give to the broken-hearted person?

A. _______________________

Hint- Keep walking away.

It's true that we all love to eat,
but they can also be great punny treats!

________ for your thoughts?

It's ________ Weekend is here!

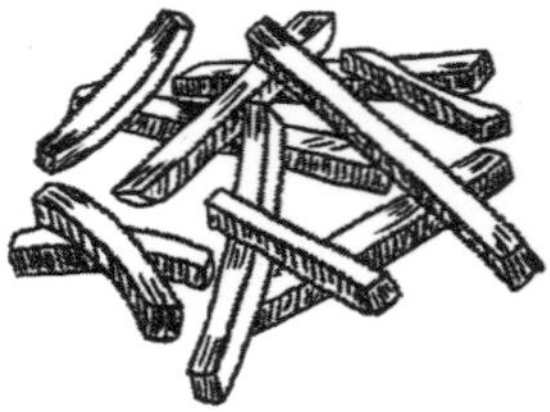

We are ________ to be together.

________ the roof. Yay!

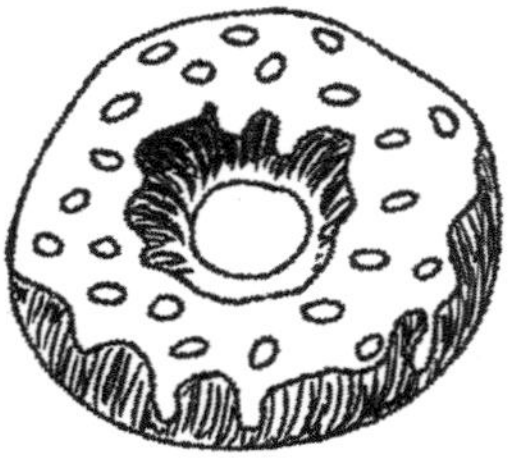

__________ worry. Everything will be alright.

__________ you.

I am kind of a big __________.

We're a great __________.

Are you confident about your sense of puns? Read these sentences and doodle your interpretations, it's your turn!

I'm a little chilli.

you're just my type.

Turn around for a break

Let the hawk-ward situations fly over your head,
complete the illustration below instead.

Let your pen or pencil fly on the page.

And doodle something here.

Are you in a snappy mood?
Doodle on the camera, don't be rude.

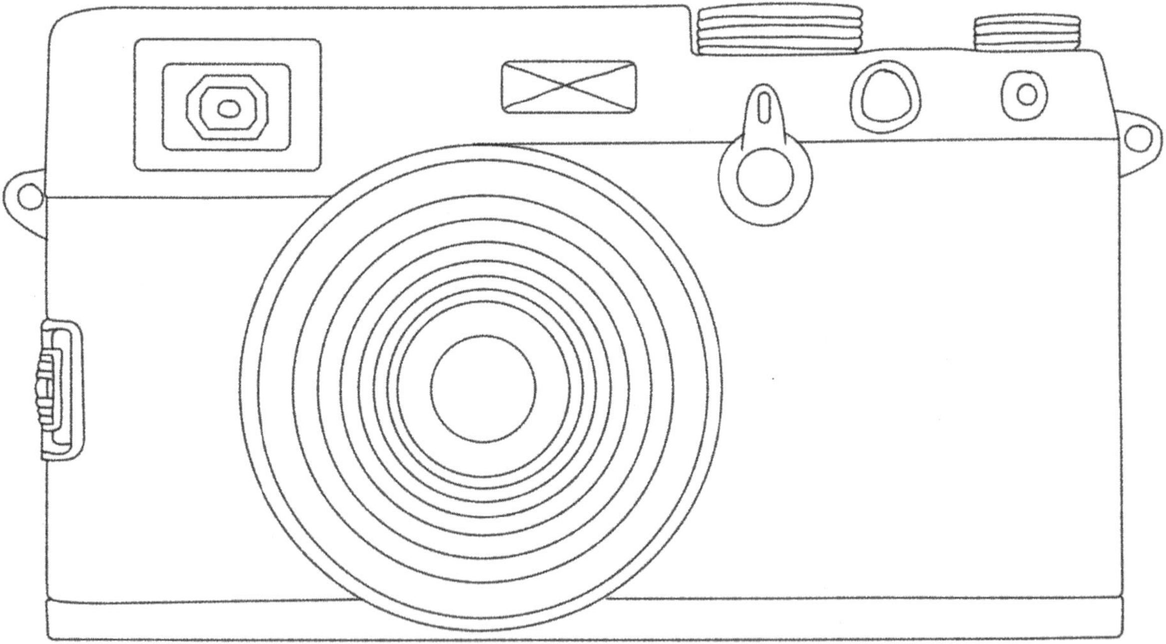

Every sentence has a pun,
circle them here just for fun.

1. After hours of waiting for the bowling alley to open, we finally got the ball rolling.
2. Always trust a glue salesman. They tend to stick to their word.
3. Every calendar's days are numbered.
4. No matter how much you push the envelope, it will still be stationery.
5. An optimist's blood type is always B-positive.
6. Reading while sunbathing makes you well-red.

Keeping a job can be a tough business, add a spot of humor to drive away the gloominess.

It was a shock when I lost my job as a psychic. I did not __________ that coming.

I had a good job working for a pool maintenance company but I had to leave it – it was too __________.

At the shoe shop, I tried for a long time but I just didn't __________ in.

My brother had to leave his job as a doctor because he doesn't have any __________.

I liked sewing things so I became a tailor but I just wasn't ________ for it.

I left my job as a historian when I realized there was no ________ in it.

I used to be a Velcro salesman but it was so boring, I couldn't ________ with it.

I was interning at a bank, but then I lost ________.

What do you call an owl that does magic tricks?

Hoodini!

What would this retro camera say,
if pun and humor would hold sway?

What happens after you take people's photos?

Then, I take them in the ____________ room and ____________ them up.

What do you like to do?

I love to ____________ people.

Is it a positive experience?

No, it is a ____________ experience.

I am so tired,
I feel like taking a rest.

You look angry!
Are you okay?

But, don't lose ____________.

Oh! I will ____________ out of it!

Have you met
your replacement?
Do you like it?

I have met my
replacement,
and we both
____________.

The kinds of puns are listed below, find them in the grid, don't be slow.

Kind of puns to look for:

HOMOPHONIC puns make use of homonyms—words that sound the same, but have different meanings.

HOMOGRAPHIC puns make use of words that have the same spelling but are pronounced differently.

HOMONYMIC puns involve using a word that has two different meanings.

COMPOUND puns are puns which involve more than one pun.

RECURSIVE puns require one to understand the first half of the pun to understand the second half.

A	H	W	E	W	Z	N	E	V	U	N	Q	B
Y	O	R	E	C	U	R	S	I	V	E	O	O
M	M	J	H	W	D	J	N	Q	B	V	U	L
H	O	M	O	G	R	A	P	H	I	C	O	O
E	P	J	M	V	U	L	Q	B	V	W	D	J
V	H	C	O	M	P	O	U	N	D	C	N	S
O	O	X	N	W	D	J	V	U	L	V	U	L
W	N	G	Y	U	L	W	D	J	O	W	E	W
Q	I	V	M	C	E	V	D	D	J	C	E	V
C	C	Y	I	W	D	J	N	N	S	N	Q	B
H	H	J	C	N	Q	B	W	E	W	Z	N	E

Turn around for a break

Loving Math is not a sine of madness,
solve this sudoku and
drive away your sadness.

8		6			3		9	
	4			1			6	8
2			8	7				
1		8			5			
	3		1					
7		5		3		9		
	2	1			7		4	
6				2		8		
	8	7	6		4			3

Bad puns are
how EYE roll

STOP! STOP! STOP!

Is your head spinning from the adpunture so far?
Unwind by solving the simple word game, superstar!

D	A	Z	Z	L		
		U	C	A		
		D	I	O		
		U	A	L		
		R	I	C		
		R	E	A		
		N	A	M		
		E	B	E		

DO YOU KNOW WHAT GOES UP AND NEVER COMES DOWN? YOUR AGE!

WISHING YOU

A  –Y

AND HAPPY

 –DAY

Don't know what card to give to your friend?
Cut out this punny card to send.

OFFSHOOT

Read the phrases below,

draw your own interpretations though.

I've got time on my hand.

Make up your mind.

The 'tree' is a part of every answer, use this clue and solve the puns faster.

1. He has committed ____________. He should be given the death penalty, sire!

2. I am sick. I need to be ____________.

3. Happy Birthday! Where's my ____________!

4. The film was too ____________ for me.

5 This is an

__________ colony.

6 I need to go to some __________ and get some well-deserved rest.

7 Diamonds are made from coal under

__________ pressure.

8 Oh no! I accidentally deleted my folder. How can I __________ it?

Grass grows by inches and dies by feet.

Do you consider yourself the pun wizard?
Then write some down, it shouldn't be hard.

Turn around for a break

Guess you need to give others a break too.

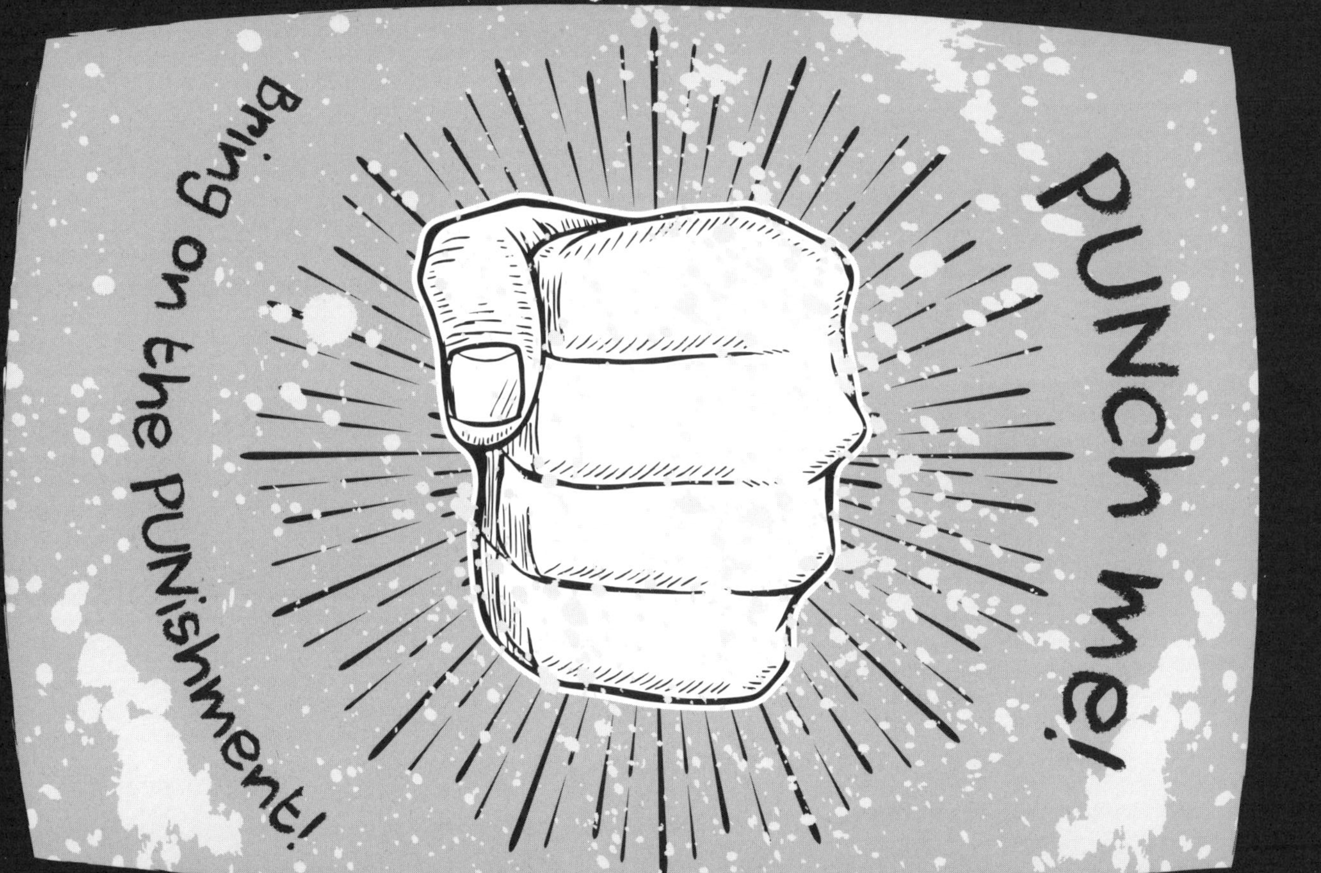

And it may hurt you.
OUCH!

Didn't get your fill from the previous bout of pranking?
Cut out more of these terrible puns for 'gifting'!

When the astronaut broke the law of gravity,
he earned a suspended sentence.

When the baker's shop burned down,
his business became toast!

Karl Marx liked herbal tea,
because all the proper-tea was theft according to him.

A flirtatious philosopher is
called a Socratease.

What kind of lighting did Noah's ark have?
Flood lights

Why couldn't the Egyptian mummy answer the call?
It was all tied up.

Michelangelo's David is considered superior to any
postmodern sculpture. It is an arty fact!

The communist failed at school, because he got
bad Marx.

Socrates' worst student was
called Mediocrities.

Vincent Van Gogh's favorite swimming technique
was the brushstroke.

OFFSHOOT

OFFSHOOT

OFFSHOOT

OFFSHOOT

OFFSHOOT

OFFSHOOT

OFFSHOOT

OFFSHOOT

OFFSHOOT

OFFSHOOT

Loving someone may be easy, but declaring it is awful tricky, guess this pun-filled note, and write one of your own quickly!

Dear ________________,

When I first met you, I knew that you were

-sactly what I was looking for. Your sense

of humor  me up! I think we make a

great .  be mine! I love you from

my head !

Yours,

____

The wheel is a mystery,
solve it to complete the quotes and taste victory!

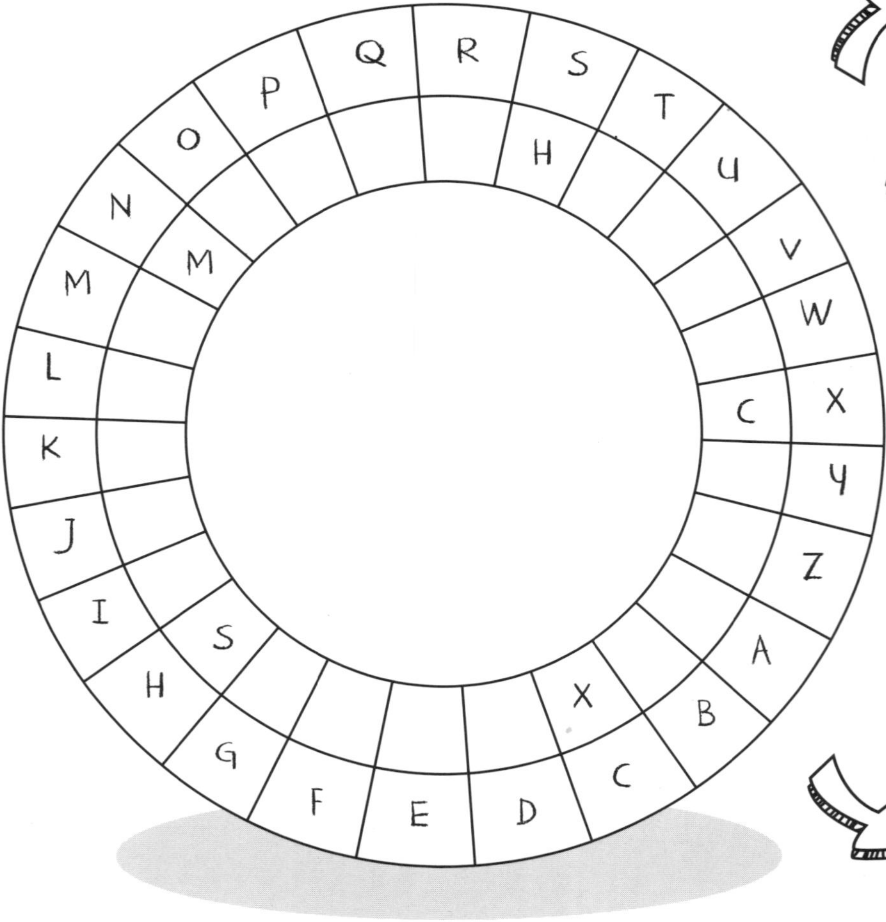

1. "You can tune a guitar, but you can't fish. Unless of course, you play

Y	Z	H	H

." - Douglas Adams

2. "Hanging is too good for a man who makes puns; he should be

W	I	Z	D	M

and

J	F	L	G	V	W

." - Fred Allen

3. "

W	V	M	R	Z	O

ain't just a river in Egypt." - Mark Twain

4. "Atheism is a

			-							
M	L	M	-	K	I	L	K	S	V	G

institution" - George Carlin

5. "I saw a documentary on how ships are kept together.

I	R	E	V	G	R	M	T

!" - Stewart Francis

Some wonderful puns are in the world of games.
Think a bit and come up with the names.

Why did the baseball players decide to play with oranges instead of balls?

To add ________ in their games

Why did the injured person refuse to talk about gym workouts?

It was a ________ subject.

What do the fans think about a high scoring football game?

Those games can be very ________.

What does refusing to go to gym count as?

________ training.

The pages of a book should not be folded,
doodle your own bookmark, go ahead, break the mold.

OFFSHOOT

Take a break, have a cut-out.

Cut it carefully.

The triangle has points to prove,
indulge in this word game on the move.

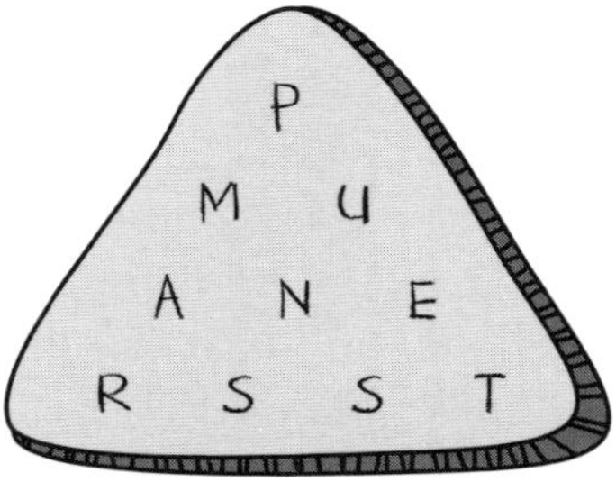

One side of triangle

Other side of triangle

Using any number of letters

Using all letters in triangle

Literary puns are the order of the day, fill in the blanks with the help of pictures, what say?

1. Who is Brontè? She's like a breath of fresh ______________.

2. Never read Fitzgerald? You have ______________ kidding me!

3. What makes 'Civil Disobedience' such a great essay?

______________ editing.

4. E.B. White's Charlotte was the original ________________ blogger.

5. Is there a pond on the animal farm, or________________?

These puns are so out of this world, think space-iously, let your thoughts unfurl.

1. What is an astronaut's favorite kind of chocolate?

_________ bars

2. Why did the Sun go to school?

To get _________!

3. How do you put a baby alien to sleep?

You _________.

4. How do you plan a party in space?

You _________.

5. What did Earth say to the other planets in the solar system?
You have no ________.

6. Where do the planets get their playlist from?
From ________!

7. Why did the people not like the restaurant on the moon?
Because there was no ________.

8. What happens when the Earth completes one rotation?
It makes everyone's ________.

Did you see something even remotely pun-ish?
Click photos and paste them here,
even if they are rubbish.

Turn around for a break

If you're a pun master you do believe
then tear this badge and wear it on your sleeve.

Enough of paper talk, now tear this out.

Cut it out nicely, o wise one!

Look at the illustration and write the pun,
They are easy and they are fun!

1

2

3

4

Are your puns making people feel low?
Write your woes with puns in the space given below!

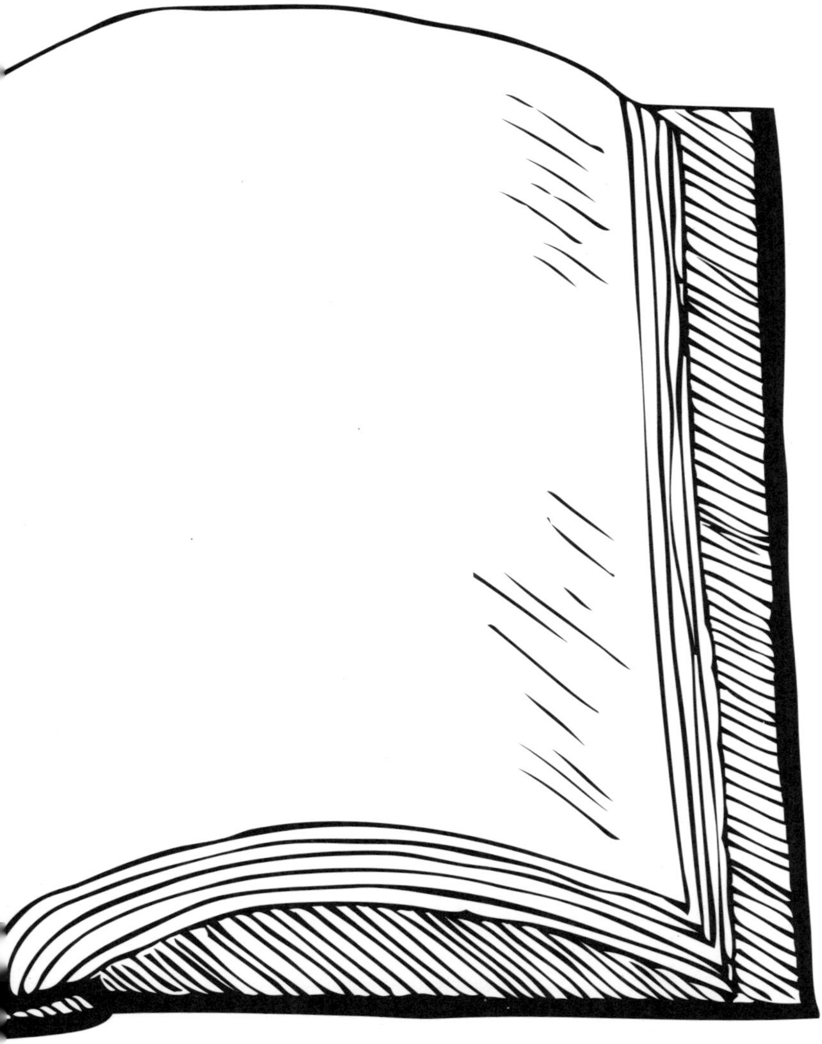

Bugs, insects and creepy crawlies are all the same,
why not figure out the puns and win the game?

Which kind of bee cannot make up its mind? ____________

What would you call a bee who is having a bad hair day? ____________

Where do bugs go to shop?

The ____________ market.

Which bee was swatted and still flew? ____________

Why are frogs always happy?
Because they eat what ________ them.

Why was the lady firefly unhappy?
Because her husband was a little ________.

What does one need to do if a bug enters the laptop?
________ the laptop.

What happened to the two bedbugs who fell in love?
They decided to get married in the ________.

Poetry can be both powerful and moving, puns about poems will leave you grooving.

1. __________ poetry was famous in the USA during 1940s.

Hint: One dances to them.

2. Yes, puns are terrible, but poetry can be __________.

Hint: A step ahead than 'bad'.

3. The reluctant poet will write __________.

Hint: Definitely not poetry.

4. When fiction writers write poetry, they are called __________.

Hint: They love to show-off their fake achievements.

5. Which Greek poetry can make a student fall sick?

The ______________.

Hint: It is written by Homer.

6. What can a poet write backward?

______________.

Hint: A portion of poetry.

7. An ode dedicated to one's limb can be called ______________.

Hint: It has five lines and rhymes.

8. Shakespeare would ______________ his enemies to vanquish them.

Hint: A poetic and devastating justice.

Wizard of pun, flaunt your talent on social media, follow the instruction below to create memes, in this space draft your ideas

Instructions

1) Research: Observe and take notes of the memes available on social media, such as viral photos/videos, trending topics and so on.
2) Gather content: Choose a topic (from the trending ones), draft your opinion and choose a medium (photo/video/create your own character). Keep the message short, simple and funny, as online attention span is short.
3) Find the necessary tools: The net has meme generators, and one can also take help from the many software available.
4) Share and repeat: Share the meme on social media and repeat the process.

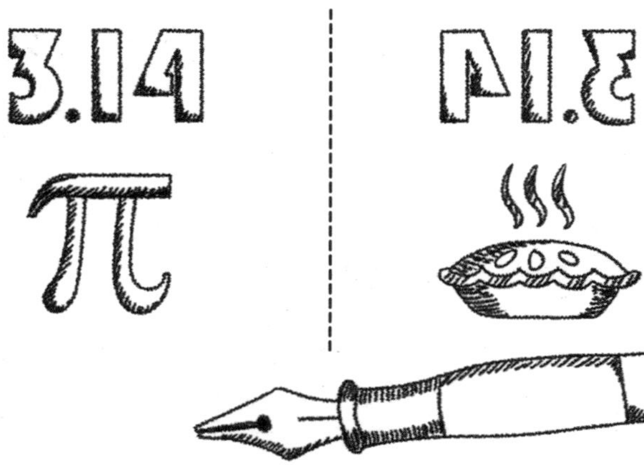

Click photos of all the puns you see,
paste and post them, fun it will be.

Turn around for a break

Your eyes need a rest,
cut-out the eyemask for sleep which is best

Your eyes must be tired of puns so get some rest.

Sleep tight.

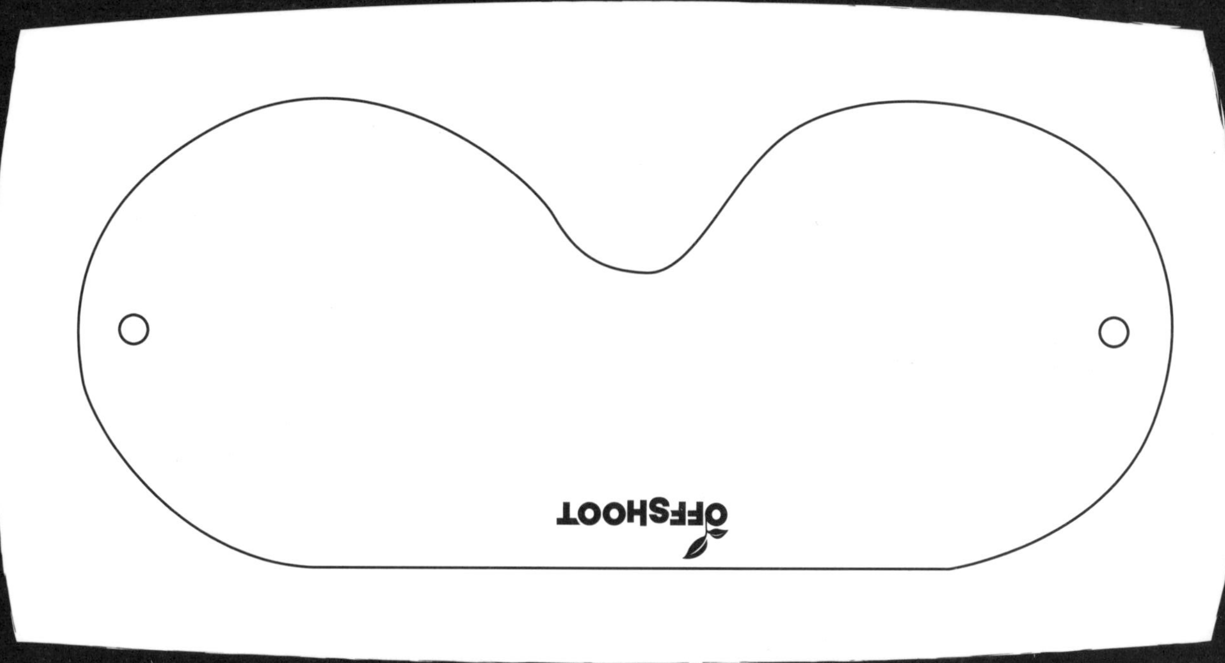

Want to up your pun games and have fun?
Cut out the strips and delight people with the terribly tearable puns!

Two crows sat on a wire together.
It was an attempted murder.

Why were people scared of the vampire snowman?
It gave frost bites!

What happens when a skater falls down during winter? The ice cracks up!

Even when the river had a nice bed it refused to stop running.

What was the water told when it came to a boil in the pan? You will be mist.

I saw a broken elevator. So, I could only stair.

Believe it or not, life seems pointless without geometry.

Why did the bike refuse to stand on its own?
Because it was two tired.

I lost my watch, but I had the time to look for it.

I had forgotten how to throw a boomerang, so I waited. It eventually came back to me.

OFFSHOOT

OFFSHOOT

OFFSHOOT

OFFSHOOT

OFFSHOOT

OFFSHOOT

OFFSHOOT

OFFSHOOT

OFFSHOOT

OFFSHOOT

Visual puns are a treat,
solve them, it'll be a feat.

1.

2.

3.

4.

Punchlines make for the best kind of laugh,
Match the lines with their other half.

1 The chemist died suddenly.

2 The two worms raced each other.

3 I used to fear all the bumps and hurdles in my life.

4 The electrician is very good.

5 The masseuse was fired from the spa.

6 The woman treated her home as a castle.

7 The man wanted to communicate with the fish in the river.

8 The man loves to gossip.

- a He decided to drop them a line.
- b Because she rubbed her clients the wrong way.
- c In a manor of speaking.
- d But I got over them.
- e His colleagues decided to barium.
- f But they ended up in a tie.
- g After all, he has a great sense of rumor.
- h He is bright and knows what's watt.

A mine of emotions is your mind,
write a punny poem and have it mined.

Turn around for a break

Take a break to brake the routine,
draw on the page while you drink caffeine.

Pause. Stop. Breathe.

Blindly move the pen/pencil on the page.

And doodle something here.

Pun is part of the word,
use the clues wisely, don't be absurd.

Deflated tyres - ______________________

Made at home, ordinary stuff - ______________________

A few words to express something strong - ______________________

A Chinese doctor using needles to cure maladies - ______________________

70s-80s rock music genre - ______________________

These puns are quite hill-arious.
Take on the challenge, the reward will be nefarious.

1. The ice cube asked its predecessor, " ______ you doing?"

2. When a woman sees her first gray hair, she usually thinks she'll ______.

3. Once the whole left side was cut off a guy! He's all ______ now.

4. When the waiter spilled a drink on a man's shirt. The man said, "This one is ______ me."

5. A visit to the cashew factory proves that it was ______!

6. A young man went to the butcher's the other day and bet him 50 bucks that he couldn't reach the meat on the top shelf. He said, "No, the ____________ are too high."

7. A client at the butcher shop was tired and finally said, "This '____________ way too long!"

8. Two fish swim into a concrete wall. Then one turns to the other and says, "____________!"

9. What did the library card say to peeve off the book? I'm ____________ you out!

10. A thief was sentenced after stealing a calendar. He received ____________ months.

Sportsmen too can be punny,
so what if they sound too funny?

SPORT

What kind of tea do hockey and soccer players drink?

____

What part of a soccer ground never stays the same?

____

Why do marathon runners make good students?
Because education pays off in the long ______________!

How many golfers does it take to change a light bulb?

_______________!

What is every runner's favorite subject in school?

_______________-raphy!

PUNS

What do a hockey player and a magician have in common?

Both can do ______________!

What did the competitor decide to do for the stair climbing competition?

He decided to ______________ his game.

Why did the golfer wear two pairs of pants?

In case he got a ______________.

The letter feels lost without a stamp,
fill it with comforting words, champ!

Turn around for a break

Before you collapse into exhaustion, take a break of caution.

We are sure you must be frustrated,
tear it into pieces you'll feel less agitated.

Or you can burn it too,
it'll be good for you.

Or choose a more fiery action.

Read these sentences carefully, circle the pun only.

1. The bald man was possessive about his comb, and he wouldn't part with it.
2. A door is not a door if it's a jar.
3. If a pirate gets his ears pierced, it costs him a buck an ear.
4. A room full of married people seems empty, because there isn't a single person in it.
5. The leopard couldn't go on a vacation, as he had trouble finding a spot.
6. When two ships carrying blue and red paint collided, the sailors were marooned.

Math class has always made your mind spin, but these puzzles will make you grin!

What did the triangle say to the circle?

you're ______________.

What did the abacus have to say about himself?

you can ______________ on me.

Why was 6 afraid of 7?

Because 7 ______________ 9.

But why did 7 eat 9?

Because you're suppose to have ______________ meals a day.

What did the Math book ask the self-help book?

You think only you have ________________?

Why is the obtuse angle always wrong?

Because, it's never ________________.

Why do mathematicians like taking walks in the park?

Because they like all the natural ________________.

What did the complimentary triangle tell the smallest triangle?

You're ________________ triangle.

These puns are filled with wisdom, and are a hoot! Beware! The clues may fly over your head saying, 'Toot, toot!'

We can brainstorm and find a solution for this ________.

Trust me, everything will be ________.

Is there any ________ way of achieving this goal?

My friend was an ________ in school. But, right now he is stuck in some dead-end job.

F. Scott Fitzgerald is my ________ favorite author.

A pun here and a pun there,
Fill the blanks with puns, they are everywhere.

A feisty person - ____________________

Fight! Hit! Fight! - ____________________

OMG! Or OMG. - ____________________

Stink; bad smell - ____________________

A weak person - ____________________

Cotton candy ingredient - ____________________

Turn around for a break

Time to take out a little bit of the frustration.

Make a list of all the people who made fun of you,
take your time and think it through.

The name which is on top of the list,
write a letter to him/her, don't resist

And put your

Animal puns, did you say?
Toucan play this game, okay?

No need to be sheepish about the fact that ________________ like puns.

When the horse asked his son to speak up, the son said that he was a little ________________.

The doe started writing her diary entry with the words, '________________, diary'.

The wild pig always laughed at puns, because he never found them ________________-ing.

But the elk didn't laugh at puns, as he didn't find them a-________________-ing.

Departed souls too have a dose of fun, fill in with words that are a pun.

1. Why is Latin the preferred language for the ghosts?
Because it's a ________ language.

2. What did one ghost say to the other when it refused to hear any puns on ghosts?
That's the ________.

3. Why are ghosts bad liars?
Because one can ________ right through them.

4. Why did the girl think that sensor doors were operated by ghosts?
Because ________ is dead.

5

How can a ghost lose weight?

By ________.

6

What is the ghost's favorite dessert?

____

7

Which felony did the ghost commit to be put in jail?

________.

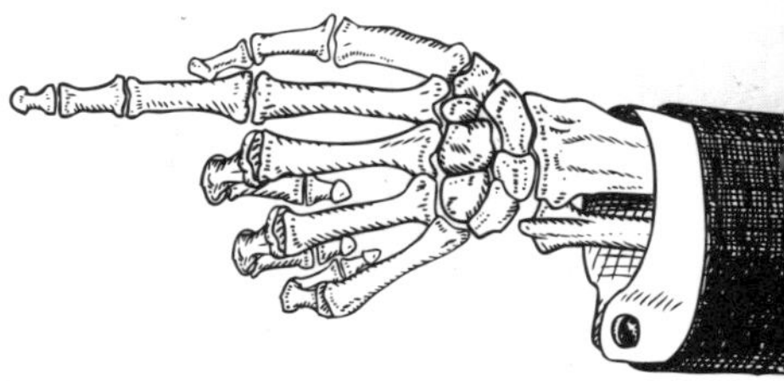

8

Why was the ghost happy to return to his old town?

He could visit his old

________.

Tablets and laptops are an indispensable part of your life.
Guess the answer to each, as into the pool of puns you dive!

The lumberjack loved ______________ in to his computer.

The difference between the car salesman and the computer salesman is that the car salesman can ______________.

Spiders love computers because they can make ______________.

Elephants don't like computers because they are afraid of the ____________________.

I could not find 'Esc' on the keyboard, so I lost ____________________.

I tried to use an app while driving but it kept ____________________.

He opened many ____________________, but was unable to let any air into the room.

Load more puns to your dead-ly arsenal, fill in the blanks to make them more discernible.

Oysters don't share because they are ________.

The Arctic circle refused to meet Antarctica, because they are ________ opposites.

Photons move faster, as they travel ________.

The man stayed up the whole night to see where the Sun went, and then it ________ on him.

The conductor got a shock, when the orchestra went ________.

Which bar do astronauts love to hang out in?

A space bar.

The energized bunny was arrested and charged with ____________.

The man tried to catch some steam, but he ____________.

The man said that he could stop anytime he wanted because he was addicted to ____________ fluid.

The people in the pub declared that the jokes about Germany were the ____________.

The kids feared the field trip to the soft drink factory, because they thought that their teacher would give them a ____________ quiz.

Hope this book helped you pun-up your game, write about your experience of the same.

Answers

Pages 4-5

soy+no+graph+her=**sonographer**
plum+bear=**plumber**
pie+law+T=**pilot**
sea+wheel Inn+gene+ear=**civil engineer**
axe+cow+tent=**accountant**
G+oh+log+east=**Geologist**
cells+pear+sun=**salesperson**
sole+deer=**soldier**

Page 6

Across
2- RIGHT – (5) WRITE
3- THERE – (5) THEIR
4- HEAR – (4) HERE
7- MEAT – (4) MEET

Down
1- WHICH – (5) WITCH
2- HOLE – (5) WHOLE
5- ATE – (5) EIGHT
6- DEER – (4) DEAR

Page 7

Page 8

Page 9

SPUN
PUNISH
EXPUNGE
COMPUNCTION
ACUPUNCTURE
PUNCTUATION
CYBERPUNK
PUNCTUAL

Pages 12-13

Shoe repair shop
Maternity room
Electricity company
Restaurant
Eye clinic
Car insurance company

Page 14

P	W	L	W	Q	B	P	X	A	P	A	M
T	G	I	O	A	M	U	U	B	X	D	J
R	E	P	T	I	N	N	U	E	N	D	O
R	Y	G	P	T	P	B	E	N	G	W	K
Q	E	D	P	P	I	P	P	D	T	I	E
Q	U	I	B	B	L	E	P	L	P	T	B
U	W	E	R	T	Y	U	I	P	P	T	C
I	S	D	F	D	H	G	B	S	B	I	F
P	X	C	B	S	N	D	N	N	M	C	D
T	O	M	F	O	O	L	E	R	Y	I	A
P	A	A	L	P	A	F	A	M	D	S	P
W	I	S	E	C	R	A	C	K	P	M	B

Pages 20-21

1. Screw up
2. Couch Potato
3. Hang out
4. Pig out
5. Down to earth

Page 22

1. Sunset
2. Bison
3. It goes back four seconds
4. Where's pop-corn?
5. Swing
6. Because they have a lot of fans.

Page 24

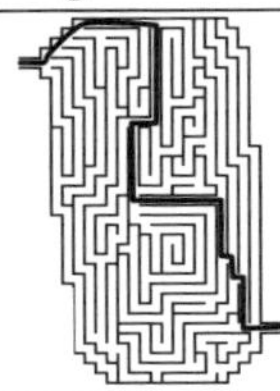

Page 25

down	pulls you
uplifiting	masses
weighing	space
drift	break the law

Page 33

Pages 26-27

1. tense
2. possessive
3. Thesaurus
4. sentenced
5. Metaphor
6. claws, pause
7. pronoun

Pages 28-29

A	26	H	19
B	25	I	18
C	24	J	17
D	23	K	16
E	22	L	15
F	21	M	14
G	20	N	13

O	12	V	5
P	11	W	4
Q	10	X	3
R	9	Y	2
S	8	Z	1
T	7		
U	6		

To be, or not to be?
That is the question

You have dancing shoes
With nimble soles.
I have a soul of lead

Pages 34-35

1. e
2. c
3. f
4. d
5. b
6. g
7. h
8. a

Pages 36-37

Peas	whale
Lettuce	board
Accordion	taco
loaf	porpoise
Thyme	otter
Seal	beet

Page 38

Across

1- STAIRS – (5) STARES
2- ROLL – (4) ROLE
4- WEATHER – (7) WHETHER
5- PEACE – (5) PIECE
6- NOT – (4) KNOT

Down

1- CELLAR – (6) SELLER
3- FLEA – (4) FLEE
4- WEAK – (4) WEEK

Page 39

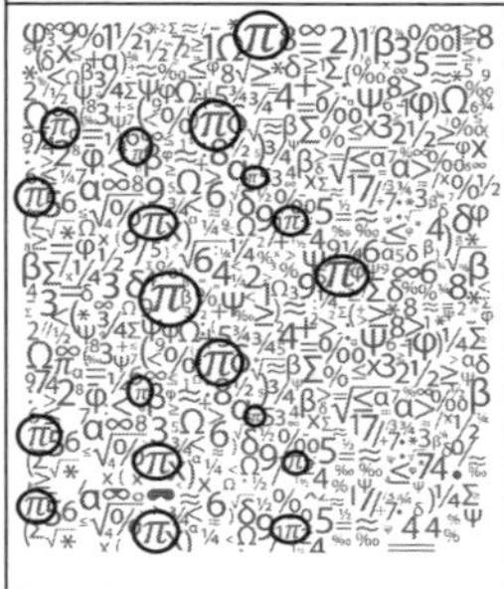

Page 43

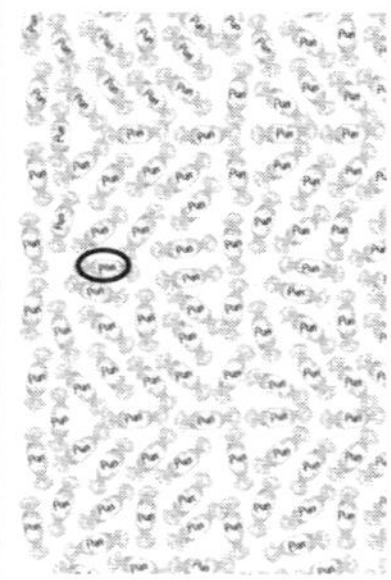

Pages 44-45

Orange
red
blue
green
gray
voilet
teal
black

Page 46

Page 47

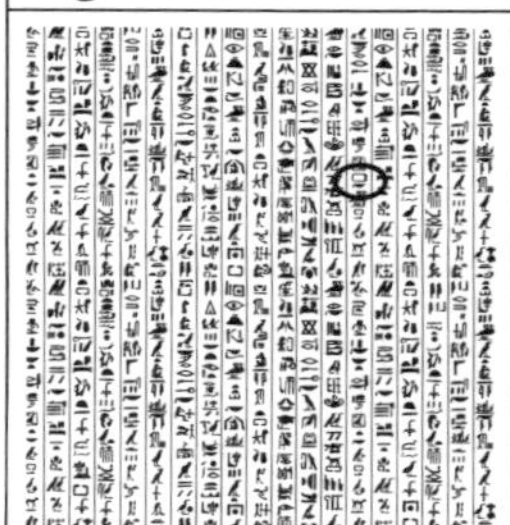

Page 48

Pages 50-51

1. drafts
2. stop
3. builds
4. appendix
5. single greatest
6. there

Pages 52-53

1. PLAIN
2. BOARD
3. FINED
4. THEY'RE
5. YOU'RE
6. BUY
7. TOWED
8. MIND
9. BREAK

Page 54

OK
OMG
NO
Na
OK2
HO
noble

Page 56

Pages 58-59

lute
drum-sticks
Cs
Pop
key
trebled
Orca-astra

Pages 60-61

Hungary, Ghana
Czech, Turkey

Finnish
Russia

Norway
Bolivia

Kenya, Denmark
Spain, Iran

Page 62

A	H	I	E	W	Z	N	E	V	A	B	S	W
P	M	D	S	Q	E	F	C	A	M	D	P	O
M	H	E	H	V	D	R	N	Q	B	W	E	M
B	O	O	T	G	E	R	P	H	I	V	E	B
E	P	P	M	A	U	O	Q	B	G	I	C	I
Z	H	H	G	O	P	R	U	N	U	P	H	N
Y	C	O	V	W	N	H	V	U	O	E	E	A
Z	Q	N	Y	W	L	Y	O	J	U	G	R	T
I	O	E	M	C	A	V	M	R	S	Y	R	I
M	E	T	O	N	Y	M	N	S	I	N	O	O
B	A	N	T	E	R	B	W	E	S	C	R	N

Page 63

5	7	3	1	8	6	4	9	2
1	6	2	5	9	4	7	3	8
8	4	9	7	3	2	5	1	6
4	5	1	6	2	7	9	8	3
3	9	6	8	5	1	2	4	7
7	2	8	3	4	9	1	6	5
2	1	7	9	6	3	8	5	4
6	8	4	2	1	5	3	7	9
9	3	5	4	7	8	6	2	1

Page 64

376

PENCILS

Page 65

Seas
waves
tide
pier
shellfish
seal-ly
shore
Sea

Page 67

LIFE
LIFT
LIST
LOST

Page 70

1. developed
2. struck
3. couldn't find
4. drill
5. raise the roof
6. hard to beat

Page 73

LIFE
LIKE
BIKE
BAKE

Pages 74-75

Ground Beef
moo-vies
Moo-dy
bull-dozer
udder
De-Calfenated
Bullogna
Moove on

Pages 76-77

Penne
Fry-day
mint
Raisin
Donut
Olive
dill
pear

Page 81

1. ball rolling
2. stick
3. numbered
4. stationery
5. B-positive
6. well-red

Pages 82-83

see
draining
patience
fit
suited
future
stick
interest

Pages 84-85

dark, blow
shoot
negative
focus
snap
click

Page 86

A	H	W	E	W	Z	N	E	V	U	N	Q	B
Y	O	R	E	C	U	R	S	I	V	E	O	O
M	M	J	H	W	D	J	N	Q	B	V	U	L
H	O	M	O	G	R	A	P	H	I	C	O	O
E	P	J	M	V	U	L	Q	B	V	W	D	J
V	H	C	O	M	P	O	U	N	D	C	N	S
O	O	X	N	W	D	J	V	U	L	V	U	L
W	N	G	Y	U	L	W	D	J	O	W	E	W
Q	I	V	M	C	E	V	D	D	J	C	E	V
C	C	Y	I	W	D	J	N	N	S	N	Q	B
H	H	J	C	N	Q	B	W	E	W	Z	N	E

Page 87

8	7	6	5	4	3	1	9	2
5	4	3	2	1	9	7	6	8
2	1	9	8	7	6	4	3	5
1	9	8	7	6	5	3	2	4
4	3	2	1	9	8	6	5	7
7	6	5	4	3	2	9	8	1
3	2	1	9	8	7	5	4	6
6	5	4	3	2	1	8	7	9
9	8	7	6	5	4	2	1	3

Page 88

DAZZLED
EDUCATE
TEDIOUS
USUALLY
LYRICAL
ALREADY
DYNAMIC
ICEBERG

Pages 92-93

1. treeson
2. treeted
3. treet
4. mainstreem
5. industreeal
6. retreet
7. treemendous
8. retreeve

Page 99

egg
crack
pear
Peas
to-ma-toes

Pages 100-101

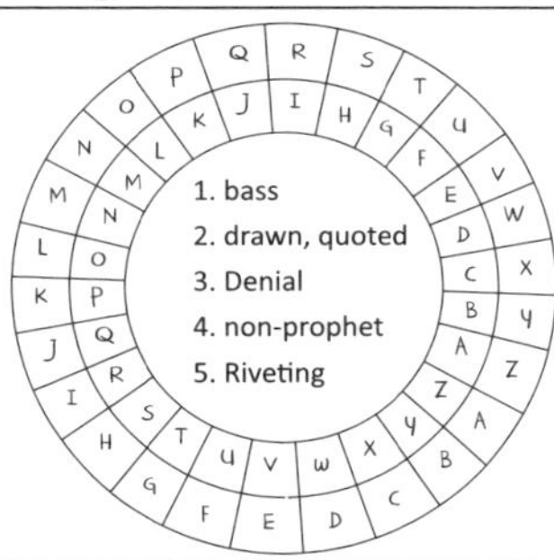

1. bass
2. drawn, quoted
3. Denial
4. non-prophet
5. Riveting

Page 102

Zest
sore
offensive
Resistance

Pages 106-107

1. Eyre
2. Gatsby
3. Thoreau
4. web
5. well

Pages 108-109

1. Mars	5. life
2. brighter	6. Neptune
3. rocket	7. atmosphere
4. planet	8. day

Page 113

FRUIT PUNCH
PHOTO BUG
TIME'S UP
CORN DOG

Pages 116-117

Maybee
Frisbee
flea
Zombee
bugs
dim
Debug
spring

Pages 118-119

1. Beat
2. verse
3. averse
4. prosers
5. Illiad
6. in-verse
7. limbericks
8. bombard

Page 127

MAIL MAN
BUTTER FLY
FIREMAN
BOOK WORM

Pages 128-129

1. e	5. b
2. f	6. c
3. d	7. a
4. h	8. g

Page 133

Punctured
Homespun
Punchy
Acupuncturist
Punk

Pages 134-135

1. Water	6. steaks
2. dye	7. steaking
3. right	8. Dam
4. on	9. checking
5. nuts	10. twelve

Pages 136-137

Penal-tea
Changing room
run
Fore
Jog
hat-tricks
step up
hole in one

Page 141

1. Part
2. a-jar
3. buck-an-ear
4. single
5. spot
6. marooned

Pages 142-143

pointless
count
eight
3^2
problems
right
logs
acute

Pages 144-145

owl-ways
owl-ready
owl-most
owl-together
owl-ternate
owl-right
owl-rounder
owl-time

Page 146

Spunky
Punch
Punctuation
Pungent
Puny
spun sugar

Page 149

ewe
horse
Deer
boar
moose

Pages 150-151

1. dead
2. spirit
3. see
4. chivalry
5. exorcising
6. I-scream
7. Possession
8. haunts

Pages 152-153

1. logging
2. drive
3. websites
4. mouse
5. control
6. windows
7. crashing

Pages 154-155

shellfish	battery
polar	mist
light	brake
dawned	wurst
electric	pop